MONTESSORI FROM THE START

A Complete Guide to Apply The Montessori Method at Home to Nurture a Happy, Smart and Sensible Child

Laurie Alber

© Copyright 2020 by Laurie Alber - All rights reserved.

No part of this publication may be reproduced or transmitted in any form or by any means, electronic or mechanical, including photocopying, recording, or any other information storage without the written permission of the publisher.

PART 1

A parent's Guide to Raising a Happy, Smart and Responsible Child

TABLE OF CONTENT

DESCRIPTION 7

INTRODUCTION 12

CHAPTER ONE "STIMULATE A BABY'S BRAIN" 16

CHAPTER TWO "PARENTING TIPS" 31

CHAPTER THREE "GRATITUDE & MINDFULNESS" 45

CHAPTER FOUR "DIET OF A TODDLER" 59

CHAPTER FIVE "ENCOURAGEMENT & ITS IMPACT" 70

CHAPTER SIX "SELF-EFFICACY & SELF-CONFIDENCE" 85

CHAPTER SEVEN "INTERESTS & HOBBIES" 103

CONCLUSION 117

DESCRIPTION

The foundation or the first step is the key to future goals and objectives. It is one of the most fundamental laws that apply to every category in the world. The children or toddlers are the foundation of the society, community, and the world. They are the backbone for future developments, enhancements, and achievements. Without the backbone, the world would collapse and become a barren land.

The book provides complete details for parents to enhance the cognitive potential and abilities of their children. It provides different tips for implementing the parenting techniques for better development and growth of the toddler/child. It will target the ways to stimulate a baby's brain to help the child progress in the competitive world. Moreover, the book informs the reader about the ways parenting affects brain development in toddlers.

"The best inheritance a parent can give to his children is a few minutes of his time each day." –O. A. Battista.

Parenting is the most hard-working and effort-full job on the planet. It is also the most responsible job too as the parents are building the foundation of a child; The greater, the perfect.

Furthermore, the book discusses some factors that have a great impact on the child's behavior and personality. The factors include encouragement, gratitude, and mindfulness. The book also provides a brief detail of the word self-efficacy and self-confidence. Encouragement allows the toddler to believe in himself and performs tasks with pride and full effort. Self-efficacy and self-confidence increase drastically with encouragement. In turn, the self-efficacy and self-confidence bring gratitude and mindfulness, so all the factors are linked together and had a combined impact on the child's/toddler's early brain development. All these factors contribute to an enhanced and increased development of the mind of a child/toddler.

Apart from this, the book emphasizes the diet of the children by encouraging the parents to provide the best quality, nutritious food to their toddlers/children. The book informs the reader about the reality of processed food in comparison to organic food. It also provides a case study related to the effects of processed food on children, with statistical data for greater understanding. Eating healthy food provides you with better and stronger immune and brain systems. The book insists parents eat healthy in front of toddlers for encouraging them to eat a better, real, healthy, nutritious, and honest food.

In the end, the book discusses the effects of the interests and hobbies of the children. It mentions the ways and methods to encourage the children to express themselves and become active in their social life. In the case of toddlers, it encourages the parents to note their behavior to determine their interest in a specific field.

How to raise a smart and happy child from zero to five? Let's find the answer to our question by going through "Brain Rules for Baby" and acknowledge some of the facts that can be a life-changing factor for a child or toddler.

INTRODUCTION

As the world is growing, it is becoming more and more fast, advanced, and intelligent. The degrees and education don't provide you with sufficient capabilities to stand and compete in this competitive world. It is your self-development, expertise, and personality to make you amongst the top. Nowadays, parents are striving to make their children more capable and intellectual. They spend thousands and thousands to shape their future. However, still, many children are unable to excel or compete in the race of the world. What is the reason!?

The reason is the foundation. The toddler is the prime stage for developing and enhancing cognitive potential and capabilities. Mostly, the parents ignore the stage as considering it less significant. They don't pay attention to the child's growth and nourishment. For sure, they will provide the best food but will have no other idea to boost the development procedure. Small insignificant factors can sometimes play massive roles in a person's life, so it is recommended not to ignore any part while raising your child.

"Parents are the ultimate role models for children. Every word, movement, and action affects. No other person or outside force has a greater influence on a child than the parent." –Bob Keeshan.

Parents are like molders. They can shape the child into a better human being or can turn the child into darkness. Your children reflect you, so make sure that you keep a good presentation of yourself in front of them. Encourage your child to be more creative. Tell them about the rights and wrongs in society, so they can differentiate it themselves.

The brain is the only organ not fully developed at birth. Approximately 90 percent of critical brain development happens in the first five years of life. It includes the entire region of the brain that had various fractions: from language, communication to memory to shaping. Newborn babies have the brain of a quarter of the size of the average adult brain. Incredibly, it doubles in size in the first year and keeps growing to about 80 percent of adult size by age three. Therefore, the primary years of the baby are very essential in the development of its future. The book provides awareness to the parents, so they become more cautious in the early stages of their newborns.

The first few years of life are critical in your child's brain development. Babies learn best through interaction – there is no substitute for YOU. The book provides various ways to the parents to help them in building a stronger foundation for their child in childhood. Let's explore the tips and brighten the future of our children;

CHAPTER ONE "STIMULATE A BABY'S BRAIN"

The brain is an organ that loses its potential if not used for some time. Biologically, the neurons in the brain develop with age. A separate neuron is created for each incident and memory. However, these neurons lose their connections if they haven't used it for a longer period. The process is called neurogenesis and develops in the hippocampus, responsible for long-term memory storage, learning any information, and emotion regulation of the brain. When the embryo is developing, the process of neurogenesis is crucial. The majority of neurons are created before birth. However, the process keeps ongoing in other parts of the brain throughout the lifespan.

It is very necessary to stimulate or boost the baby's brain for making it more responsive, active, creative, etc. There are numerous advantages and no disadvantages in stimulating a baby's brain. Some of the benefits of stimulation are listed below:

- **Neurological Pathways:** The most significant reason for stimulating a baby's brain is to prevent any changes in the brain structure due to stressful situations or conditions. Of course, this will leave a drastic effect on the baby's future, and there are no compromises in it. Neurological pathways are also disturbed, and to prevent it in the toddlers, parents must boost and stimulate their baby's brain.

- **Parenting & Relationship:** Parents can learn essential parenting tips while stimulating their babies' brains. They will be able to gain more experience and expertise in the field of parenting. Good Job!

It is important to establish a healthy relationship with children. Children who grow up with an insecure relationship have a negative effect on their behavior, education, physical and mental health in later stages of life.[2]

Moreover, parents will be able to develop a more interactive and healthy bond with their children. It will have a double effect on the brain's potential of both parents and children.

- **Social effects:** Stimulating the baby's brain at an early stage will help the baby in developing a successful social life in his life. He will be able to excel more in his life and will produce overwhelming results. Simulation through various senses, such as face-to-face, etc. will help the child in developing the auditory and visual senses, thinking and intelligence skills, and enhance interaction features.

Newborn babies could adapt to surroundings, quickly, and grasp things with astonishing speed. The brain of the child is very sensitive to what it experiences in an environment. Therefore, stimulation is very significant for brain development.

Everything that happens from the time they conceive that baby till their baby is born, to their first birthday, there is so many changes happening, and everything that happens in their lives affects brain development. The brain changes and grows so rapidly from the time they are born; their brain is about the size of grapefruit. By the time they go to kindergarten, it's about the size of a big cantaloupe. After this age, the brain almost grows not at all, so you are looking to make an impact from birth to five. The following bullets give suggestions to the parents in stimulating their baby's brain:

- **Give Your Baby a Good Start from Birth:** It is a parent's responsibility to provide the best of all conditions, nutrients, environment, etc. for your baby while it is implanted in the uterus (womb). Quit smoking and stop going to a place that is noisy or polluted. Smoking is not only injurious for your health but the baby too. Smoking cause preterm birth, decreased weight of the baby (low birth weight), birth defects of mouth and lip. It also causes sudden infant death syndrome (SIDS). According to the American Lung Association, 10 percent of the infants die due to smoking factor.

Apart from smoking, parents should give special attention to the drugs they are taking during pregnancy. Many drugs can be extremely dangerous for your children. Many children who were drug-abused in the womb struggles with severe learning problems and suddenly act with unprovoked aggressive behaviors.

Furthermore, eat healthy food. Try taking in more fruits and vegetables to boost the immunity of your child and yourself. The stronger the immunity, the less prone the body is to diseases. Take plenty of sleep and avoid listing to loud music. Moreover, get a massage and relaxing therapies to keep away the stress. Try reading books and solving IQ questions to make the child more intelligent and smarter.

- **Turn Up the Baby Talk:** Try interacting with your child using vocals and pitches. Respond to their voices and help them learn syllables. Read books and sing rhymes to make them aware of the words and their senses. It is a fact that infants that get interacted frequently or are living in a joint family tend to learn early. Use small picture books to allow the child to connect the pictures to different scenarios. These efforts will allow the child to develop speaking and speech skills. Pediatricians say that reading to your children is a great idea, but so is just talking to them. Babies get their greatest comfort from the human voice, and that voice is yours (parents). Keep up the parent-child dialogue by doing random talks about different daily life work. Listen to the consonants of your child and note them down; soon, this babbling will turn into words. All the actions of the child are some form of communication. For example, a smile is a way of communication that means, "Do it again! I like it." Make sure that by the age of two, your child can form two-word sentences, and you can understand 50 percent of the conversation. By the age of three, you should be able to understand 75 percent of the conversation, and your child should be able to form three-word sentences. By age four, children and parents can talk in complex sentences and understand each other fully.

- **<u>Play Games That Involve Hands</u>:** Let your child experience the interactivity of the world. Use hands to play with your child. Play games like a little piggy, patty-cake, peekaboo, puppets, etc. Learning through play will allow the child to understand better and become more indulged in the activity. Allow the child's imagination to spark while providing hilarious, interactive play. Moreover, playing through hands will allow the child to develop a sense of touch. The child will become active and will gain cognitive potential. At first, it may seem useless, but there are long-lasting effects on the development of the child's personality.

- **Build Trust by Being Attentive & Focused:** Being a parent is a tough job. You have to spare a separate concentration to keep an eye on your infant/child. It affects your daily life work, but it is a surety to gain the trust of your baby. The baby feels relaxed and happy if the parents are around and attentive. Make sure that you respond promptly when your baby cries. It will create a stronger bond and relationship. Soothe, nurture, cuddle, and reassure her so that you build positive brain circuitry in the limbic area of the brain, which is involved in emotions. Your calm holding and cuddling, and your day-to-day engagement with your baby, signal emotional security to the brain.
- **Make Meals Positive:** Make the food seasons a development for the child. How is this possible? Well, allow your child to feed himself. Don't worry about the mess as this habit will make the child more comfortable

in eating the meals. Interestingly, the child would consider it a game and would love to play, even if the food is not tasty. In this stage, make sure that you give everything to your child, so they develop a taste for all the foods. Keep note of the food they like and dislike. Make sure that the food is a balanced meal that helps the child to meet its nutrition content of the day. Making meals positive will increase the absorption rate of the child and will enhance gut functionality. The food will digest properly and will cause no bloating or constipation. All these ways will allow the child to develop a pleasant association with mealtime and eating. Nagging and battles about food, on the other hand, can lead to negative brain patterns.

- **<u>Set Up a Safe Environment for Your Crawling Baby or Toddler</u>:** The child starts crawling at the age of 9 months or a year. Baby can opt for different methods for locomotion like scooting or bottom shuffling, slithering on her stomach, etc. Very soon, the child will understand the parameters and areas in the house. The children will start developing a relationship with the objects

and will learn some vocabulary such as under, over, big, etc. He will build a comfort zone in his world or home. Parents should make sure that the comfort zone of their child is fully protected. They should add a rug on the floor for comfortable movement from place-to-place. Moreover, the connections of switches should be moved to a higher place. Tables and chairs that are having sharp corners should be removed. Parents should make sure that the baby feels happy and comfortable in his favorite area, and the environment is safe for children's locomotion.

- **Express Joy and Interest in Your Baby:** Let your body language, your shining eyes, your attentiveness to babbling and baby activities, and your gentle caresses and smiles validate the deeply lovable nature of your little one. Let them know that you are interested in their daily routine activities. In this way, the bond between the child and parent will strengthen. The baby will have a positive effect on his development and personality.

Enjoy the process of stimulation and make your child more productive and intelligent. Your initial steps will help your child in taking big steps in the future.

CHAPTER TWO "PARENTING TIPS"

There are many different types of parents, those who care and are overly possessive, and those who are not interested in their children and let them be on their own. And then, some know how to keep a perfect balance in everything. Unnecessarily, parents can be of the same type. Sometimes the father takes a lot of interest, while the mother is the opposite. If you are facing such a problem, then you must not show the other parent (gender) how you feel about them, but instead, go together to parental programs where they help you look at the problems in the development of your child. There is no denying that all parents don't love their children, but sometimes they fail to understand that children do not only require their love and money but understanding and attention too.

In the modern world of ours, it wouldn't be wrong to say that parents don't have time to take care of their children. The best possible solution is to either hire a nanny or make them stay with their grandparents for the better. But the reality is that babysitters are also responsible for about 4.2 percent of crimes on children. A babysitter or a grandmother can never give the attention to detail that a parent is willing to give in the first place.

The one advantage of both parents working is that they will be able to complete the needs of their child quite easily, but they then have no control over what their child grows up to be. If both the mother and the father are working, then they must come to an agreement where one should stay at home while the other one is gone. Or they both work the morning and at least both be there for their children for the better part of the day. Have meals together and have playing time together. The parents must take every possible chance to understand their child better, so they can take the appropriate steps to raise them perfectly. And one thing that should be kept in mind is that it's not the mother who is supposed to make all the sacrifices. The father knows as better as the mother, and his role is as important for a child's growth.

One of the most important things in child growth is their self-esteem. If you fail to put courage and confidence in your child, he will think of himself as less as compared to his friends around him and will eventually get bullied for not being better. Unnecessary bashing of the child, throwing verbal abuses at them, will only make them think less of themselves, and you have no idea how much damage that can cause. Even before starting a task they will know that is good at nothing or that someone else can do this better than them. They will never possess any good leadership qualities, and neither they will know how to handle any sort of pressure.

Even if your child has done something imperfectly, got bad grades, or performed poorly in a small quiz taken at home don't tell them that they can't do it but instead tell them they did a good job as it was their first try, and how can they improve it. Make them realize that everyone is bad in their first attempt, so they are never afraid to make any discoveries and seeking out new adventures. Tell them it is fine to be wrong because, at their age, life is only about learning from your mistakes. Tell them that the real meaning of FAIL is "the first attempt in learning."

The most controversial point in bringing up a toddler is 'how to respond to their tantrums'. This has been a very sensitive topic where everyone has different widespread opinions. Some say that you must not pay any heed to the wild tantrums of the baby, while others say that it is harsh not to do so. Well, to be honest, it's not harsh at all if you are just overly emotional. And believe me, your child will know about this as your weakness, so if your child is throwing a tantrum, you should never pay any heed to it at all. But the question arises that if a child still does not speak and is unable to tell you what he is crying about, then how are you supposed to know is it is a tantrum or not? Well, some parents go for the trial and error method. Try and feed them, check their diapers, and, if not, then let them be.

Another thing that you can do from start is to observe your child very closely in his early years, and if he takes a tumble and you know he is fine, then don't go over there picking him up and making the worst out of the situation. It's hard to do, but going over there and caressing the nonexistent wound will only make the baby more sensitive. On the other hand, let them get up on their own, and you will be amazed to know how quickly they go back to what they were doing before. Like this, they will develop a habit, and the one time they will be crying out loud, you will know that something is wrong as your child never does that.

Another thing that comes to the mind is that how do you take care of your child physically? Well, there is no denying that children are very sensitive and must be taken extra care of. The most important thing you must be careful about is that they do not fall on their headstrong or at all actually because head injuries in children can cause some serious damage and even if you think your child is fine after one observe them for any change in behavior and how they respond to things how they are making their expressions and walking etc. do this till your pediatrician's appointment because you never want to take any risk of a concussion. But that does not mean that you be extra possessive and don't let them explore at all. That is how they learn.

Another main problem which the parents tend to have is not knowing the right time for their children to start kindergarten. According to pediatricians and psychologists, the child should start going to kindergarten at the age of five. It is a mistake when parents think that their children will learn new things in kindergarten if they got their early. However, the truth is that they will only learn to interact with others, and of course, a few more things. The child learns better under the attention of two parents, rather than one teacher taking care of 20 students at once, so don't rush your child to kindergarten because the best school for him in his early years is his own home.

A toddler must learn how to potty train and you must not force them on it. Forcing a child to potty train will bear fruitful results, but it is something that a child will never understand he needs to do when he feels like being cleaned and when he wants to go there naturally himself. What some parents do is force the child to go potty even when he doesn't feel like going. It does not help at all in the development of the child. It is a feeling that the child must understand, so ask the child when he needs to go himself and then help him do it. Let them take their time there is no advantage in making them learn things forcibly.

The parents, on the other hand, must be a perfect role model for their children. If they do not respect each other in front of their child, then the toddler will follow their behavior and have no respect for his parents. The parents must communicate with each other on the problems of the child. It must not be like that the father and mother are too busy talking to each other about what problem their child is facing or maybe decide on their thinking they know better. It's always better to make a collective smart decision rather than a rash one. And of course, the same communication must be established between the child and their parent. Even if you know better in a situation it would never hurt for you to ask your child what he thinks must be done so that he should know from the start that his opinion matters even if it's something as small as where should we eat tonight?

Teach your kids how to be positive. Even if they find themselves in a mess or a problem, tell them to look on the bright side of it. Tell them not to be sad about it happening but first, look at the positive aspect and then look at how to get rid of the situation. Let them try to solve their problems on their own first and make sure you let them know that you are right with them in every situation and once they do get rid of it, give them a good reward or a round of applause to tell them that they did well. They must know that mistakes in the first place are what help you be the better version of yourself knowing what to do in each situation.

Abuse. This is something that can hurt the mind of your child even if you think he or she is too young to understand it. If you hit your child mildly, they will not understand that it is something that must not occur, and when an outsider does that to them, they will take it quietly. Hitting your child to make them learn anything is not something you should be thinking about. On the other hand, an abusive relationship between two parents is something that helps a child's mental growth. Respect each other and help your child respect others too.

Tell your son to treat other females like he 'wants' her mother and sister to be treated, and teach your daughter to treat all men like she 'wants' her father and brother to be treated.

Lastly, a child should learn about discipline. A child's discipline, outside the house, reflects the situation inside it. A child must have good etiquettes on how to sit, stand, talk, eat, and even walk for that matter. When it comes to their discipline never be emotional. They must know that this is something that will not be compromised. Ground them if there is the need to do that, but try and make sure that if they can understand by your words, then there is no need for grounding. Don't bash them right away or ask them why they did something like that, so when they won't have an answer to their mistake, make them realize by talking to them and showing them the right path.

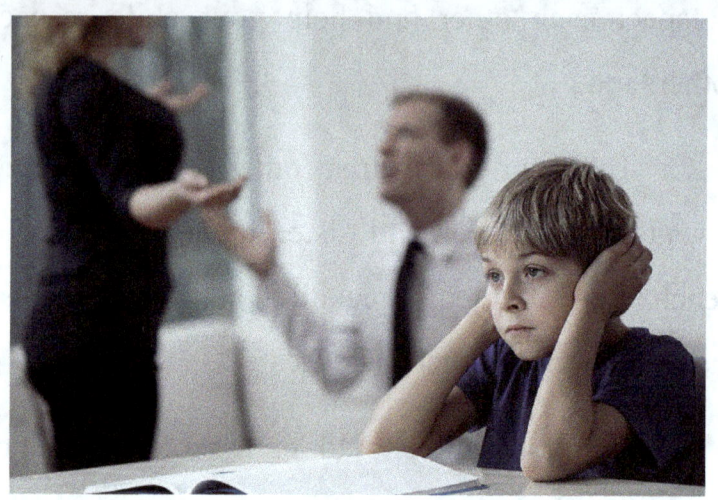

Always show them flexibility, so they know that there is always room for mistake because some children make mistakes being afraid to make them.

On the other hand, the child must know that they must be good behind parent's back too, so try and find good things they do behind you and reward them for it, so they keep doing that practice. Make sure your children know that love is unconditional and their family comes first over anything so they can never be hated.

Some parents are always stressing about why their kids haven't spoken yet or started walking yet. They start to compare their children with others of the same age who are doing similar things. And then, they start questioning their parenting and think that their child might be slow. This is wrong! Don't worry about it, don't enforce things onto your growing toddler. Remember they will learn eventually; every child learns at their own pace.

CHAPTER THREE "GRATITUDE & MINDFULNESS"

In the early years of their lives, children tend to pick many characteristics of their parents. Gratitude and mindfulness are the things that are better understood when the children observe other people doing it. For once, we must be grateful to every person around us, including the kids. The best thing about gratitude and mindfulness is that they both reinforce each other. A person in his healthy and sound mind will always be grateful.

What is gratitude? To enlighten one on it, you just need to understand its meaning. Gratitude is the feeling of gratefulness, for which you must give everyone the due credit they deserve. If you are helped by a person, you must not think lower of yourself by any means and neither feel like they are subservient to you for doing so for you.

A person not grateful will naturally come off as an arrogant one even if he does not mean to be that way. He will not appreciate the better work of people around him and always sound cocky to start with. He will always come across as a self-centered person who thinks that he is better than everyone else, but the reality is somewhat different. You can't be the master of all, and eventually, it is teamwork that makes everything run smoothly, as there should be no fighting over the fact that what is better than one's brain? Every person in his sound mind would say more than one.

Thereby, when we say a person with a sound mind would be grateful, it means a person who has awareness and knows what is happening around him will always know how important it is to show gratitude to other people. They must be of the opinion that working for you and working with you is something they can give a thought about, and in doing so, they shall be aware of the expected appreciation and will hence, give in their maximum effort. You will be surprised to know that once a person is complimented for doing work, he will always do better to get the next thing to be liked even more in order to receive even more compliments and please the people around them too.

So, if you want your child to be a great leader or to be a better person to be precise, you must show them how to be grateful and be grateful for a sense of mindfulness rather than it not hold any meaning. No one comes out of their mother's womb knowing everything, but they tend to see everything around them and set their morals according to things they like and dislike for themselves. So, when you are going to be grateful to your child, they are going to know how well it feels to be appreciated and the fact that how highly the person appreciating them is thought of. A person with a sound mind will better observe things around him. This helps the person not being biased and self-centered in situations. In fact, his judgment is no longer blurred with such clarity of thoughts.

Now that we know that showing gratitude to the people around is very important, let me emphasize the importance of being grateful for the things you have. Let me start by saying if you are perfectly healthy and can afford three meals a day and are getting an education and loved by the family and have a roof over your head. You are one lucky person as millions of people are deprived of all these basic hierarchical needs in life.

Don't ever hesitate to take your children out to show them what the real-world problems are. If you reside in a posh area, make sure to take your children to areas where people are homeless and are working by every possible means to get a roof over their heads. This will develop an inquisitive mind of the child where he/she will question you about the reason for their condition. Upon which, you can always tell them that they are no different than us and that we must be grateful for what we have and work hard to value what we own. They must be aware of the harsh realities of life and that no one chooses to live like this but those who aren't grateful for what they have will eventually end up like this since they don't even know the mere importance of what they have and can only realize it once they lose it. They must learn to live out of their comfort zones and push themselves out of those zones whenever needed.

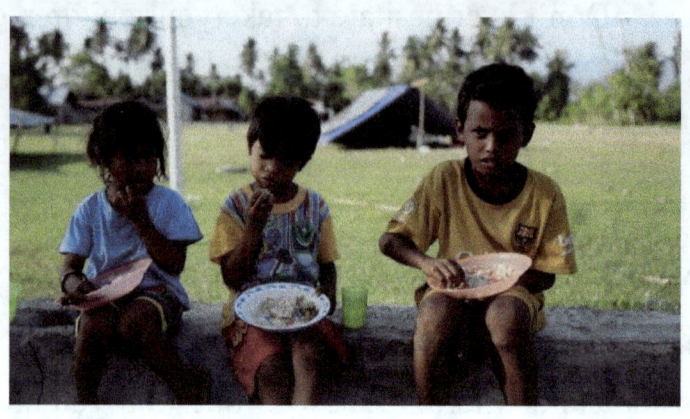

If you are a rich parent who can afford to complete all the wishes of your child, you will surely feel like a good parent giving their children whatever they want. But the harsh reality is that you are doing more damage than good. Children having everything they want with little or no effort will tend to make a habit out of it because that is what they do. They learn from experiences. Make your child work hard for what he deserves like you once did to be where you are today. Otherwise, good things you imbibed in yourself from your childhood experiences are not going to trickle down on them, and there is no better teacher than experience itself.

Award them for things rather than giving them out for free. Let them know that everything in this world comes for a price. If they want something, you must tell them that they must behave well for it to get it. If they ask you for something, don't reject it right away but tell the child if he is good, he will eventually get it and then see them work for it. If you reject their wishes right away, it will only make them stubborn and hard to deal with because then they'll know that crying is the best means to get their wishes granted. Why not use that energy to behave nicely rather than crying?

Other than that, surprise them with rewards even if they don't ask for it, so they know that good actions will never go unappreciated. If they achieve good grades, award them with something you think is appropriate for them according to their marks. What some parents do is that they give rewards to their children for achieving a very high target, but in reality, it is most needed, when your child is showing improvement, may it not be very high grades for that matter. While doing so, make sure they realize that if they had scored better, they would've been appreciated even more.

Sometimes you must make sure that your child does not get what he wants, so he can understand that he cannot always have what he wishes for even after trying their level best. You don't always get what you want, and you, more than often, must be content with what you have. Make them think and grow outside the bubble.

Grateful parents yield a grateful child. Parents must teach their children to not be biased in situations, and give people credit for what they deserve rather than having a judgmental statement. They must learn to help people and appreciate them for what they are doing praising them. This can be embedded into a child by admiring what he does right by giving them credit and telling them they did good, and if not, then they must be taught for what they did wrong. Little actions of parents such as greet and admire the gardener, the security guard, or the babysitter will help the child understand the importance of praising people. A person not given due credit for what he does will eventually give up in disappointment or frustration.

One good way of making your children learn more about the harsh realities of this world is to take them for trips around the world and show them how to be generous. Make them realize that helping people will put smiles across a lot of faces including their own.

A parent must make sure that their child knows that the monetary things in life are not important, but that how he treats others is much more important. Parents should fix certain pocket money knowing the expenses of their child, and teach them to make the best out of it just like an act of survival. You will be amazed at how ungreedily your child will develop knowledge on how he needs to get the best out of the situation.

On the other hand, mindfulness is a very important aspect of our lives, be that a child or the parents themselves. A person who is not mindful of his surroundings cannot differentiate between right and wrong, and will eventually put himself in danger by not knowing how to choose the right. To start with, your child must be given basic information on not going out with strangers or trusting them, and that no one can abuse them, and that if something of this sort happens, they must report to their parents immediately rather than being afraid to talk to them. It happens more than often that a child fails to communicate with their parents thinking that they won't get support and get scolded for putting themselves in that position in the first place. This behavior is condemnable and one must help the child in solving the problem, and eventually, he will learn not to do it again as he has already had a bad experience with it.

If your child fails to distinguish between right and wrong, he will eventually be a part of a lot of wrongdoings including bullying. Parents must keep an eye on what their child is watching, playing, what his/her company is and whether he knows what he is doing is right or wrong. I believe that a good way for a family to communicate is to eat together and talk about their daily routines where parents can assess what their children are up to and how they are dealing with their day to day tasks and the type of mentality are they developing.

Gratitude and mindfulness, when taught together, will yield much better results than what you expect. Once your child learns from you and the people around you, he will differentiate between how he feels good about something and make strong morals from it. A child who is appreciated for what he does will appreciate others as he would want people to resonate with the same feeling. The same goes for teaching him to be grateful for what he is being provided with. He should even pray and thank for the meal he is provided with.

If you look around, you will notice a trend that the children of rich parents are mostly spoiled and do not know how important it is to work for what you have as compared to the children belonging to mediocre and poor backgrounds because they know how their parents strived hard to provide for them. If your child is not mindful, your next generation is doomed to suffer as they will lose what they didn't work hard for.

A child must have gratitude to realize what he has and to practice it, he requires mindfulness.

CHAPTER FOUR "DIET OF A TODDLER"

A baby's nutrition is very important, and it must be taken extra care of. The trend that is followed nowadays is that the baby is given formula milk instead of wrong breast milk. The breast milk of a mother contains certain contents that are very healthy for a baby. Colostrum contains lactoferrin that aids the body in the fight against bacteria and viruses. It also contains antibodies mainly IgA that again helps in immune reactions and growth factors that are very essential for the baby's growth. Providing a baby formula milk may develop him as lactose intolerant, a condition in which the gut does not have enzymes to digest lactose, causing severe diarrhea and flatulence. In such cases, you must give the baby lactose-free milk formula for treatment and stay away from dairy products. You can start with semi-solid foods from the age of six months and eventually move on to cow milk after a year.

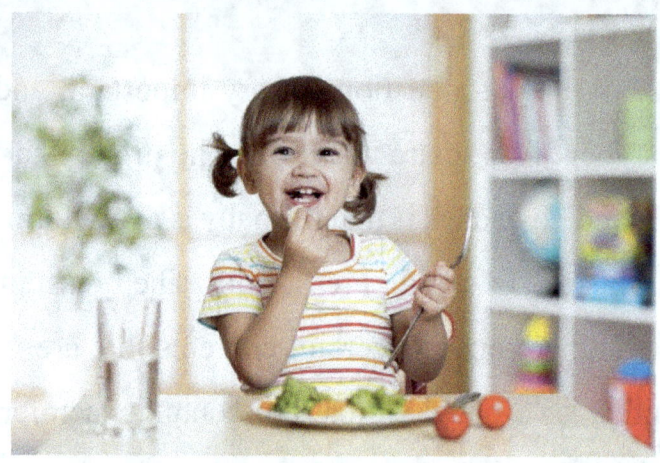

One other thing to be taken care of in front of the babies or toddlers are that the parents must eat healthier too. If you keep on binging on fast foods and sweets, the babies will eventually want to imitate and if not given, they are bound to throw tantrums your way and reject any other nutritious meal given to them. Children can be stubborn. Drinking alcohol and other beverages in front of the kids is a really bad influence on them so extra care must be taken to avoid the risk of them going on little adventures of their own behind your backs just out of curiosity.

If in the early years of life, your child becomes colic, often, it is nothing to worry about. Water with fennel seeds is a great remedy. Just take about a cup of hot water and boil fennel seeds in them, drain the water and give it to your baby by spoon. It helps with the pain. Other than that, gripe water can also be given.

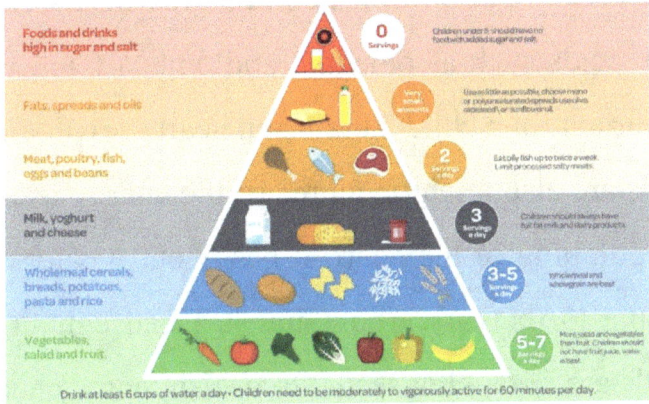

Carbohydrates are an important source of energy for the child. Bananas, apples, strawberries, vegetables, oats, brown rice, quinoa, chia seeds, pumpkin seeds, lentils, kidney beans, peas, potatoes, hazelnuts, walnuts, peanuts, and many sweets things are rich in carbohydrates. They supply about 4 calories/g and the main storage form of carbohydrates in the body is glycogen which is broken down into glucose to be supplied as an instant form of energy. The regional daily allowance of carbohydrates is 130g/day.

Lipids and fatty acids, on the other hand, are also very important for a child's growth. Essential fatty acids such as omega 3 and omega 6 are very important for a child's brain and heart growth. Fatty acids are also a major source of the energy used in the pumping of the heart. It has about 9 calories/g double to that of carbohydrates. Lipid containing foods are nuts, chia seeds, fatty fish, eggs, cheese, avocadoes, and butter. The regional daily allowance of fats for children is 25g/day. Trans fatty acids like margarine used to increase the shelf life of food are very dangerous to health as they increase the quantity of low-density lipids and decrease healthy high-density lipids causing heart problems.

However, a large number of fats must not be taken as they tend to make the child obese by depositing around the viscera and abdomen. Thus, a healthy diet must be kept in balance.

Proteins, on the other hand, are a good source of energy and help in the development of muscles. Foods containing proteins are meats, eggs, and dairy products. The regional daily allowance of proteins is 13g/day for children of 1 to 3 years. Some diseases due to deficiency in proteins are very common all around the world which includes kwashiorkor which occurs due to low protein intake. The growth is retarded with a protruding abdomen and many more problems. Another disease commonly caused by low-calorie intake is marasmus which is characterized by severe retardation with the facial appearance of an old man, a shrunken belly, weak and atrophic muscles with bodyweight less than 60 percent of normal. Hence, normal protein intake is very important in growing children as they need it for growing muscles.

Vitamins contain an adequate amount of minerals which are essential for the baby's growth and development. The fact that these are included in a balanced diet is a good way to cover their daily needs. If your child does not like to eat certain foods containing vitamins and minerals, you must find an alternate source of it as they are widespread. However, supplementation must be avoided as vitamins have certain toxic effects.

Most reactions of the body are found in an aqueous medium so extra care must be taken that your child drinks enough water each day as he must be losing a lot of it in sweating during playing and running around. A child must drink about 5 glasses or 1 liter. You must also check your child's urine often to see if it is of normal color.

On the other hand, you must be clever with how to feed your child with certain foods. Children hate vegetables so cook things they like and add healthy foods in small portions so that they do not notice it. If they don't want to eat something, don't force that onto it as it will only worsen the situation. Try being a little flexible rather than forcing them to eat. They will eventually eat it when they feel hungry.

While feeding, make sure your child is not talking a lot and sitting upright to prevent any danger of choking. If your child manages to choke himself with food, what you must do is come behind him and wrap your arm just around their diaphragm below the ribs and squeeze them tightly jerking them up while doing it to push the food out. First, you can try and pat their back and if that does not help, the above-mentioned technique is always there.

Make stuff for your children which is easier to eat and pleasant tasting. Foods can be semi-solid or even fried for an older child as they tend to enjoy such things more. Snacks are important in a child's diet as they provide the energy and some calories in between the main diets.

Colas is a big no! Fresh juices are the way to go but processed juices and foods should be avoided as they do more harm than they can do good. You must give your child occasional access to things they like, like ice cream and chocolates but not in excess as it will lead to dental cavities and obesity-related problems.

One other problem that the kids face is that they are forced to eat a lot and when they start to get overweight, they already become habitual of eating more than required. The parents then restrict them from eating which only adds on to the problems. They feel like they are not full and they still

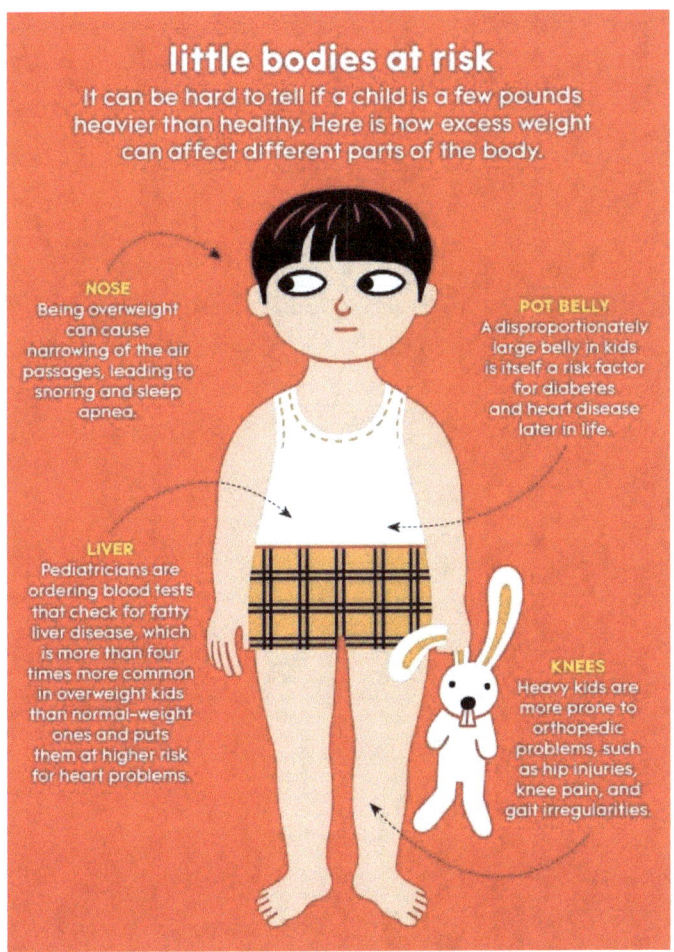

experience hunger pangs. They get irritated and will eventually affect their day to day life leading to problems at school and home too. So, care must be taken in what you feed your child and by in much quantity. Excess of everything is bad.

CHAPTER FIVE "ENCOURAGEMENT & ITS IMPACT"

The latest version of Oxford Dictionary defines "Encouragement" as an attempt to give hope, to inspire with courage or to stimulate growth. Encouragement serves as an important driving force that motivates us to either initiate or to continue an ongoing process, let it be something as minor as a school science project or something as big as life itself. Taking the example of how a body needs to be fed with nutrients, similarly, our actions need to be appreciated or acknowledged for the best outcome. Encouragement is the appreciation we need at every phase of our life, every age and to be precise, every point. An old man needs to be appreciated to help him cope with the challenges of the old life, similarly, a toddler needs to be appreciated to help him take his first step and speak his first word.

Focusing on the importance of encouragement, it must be understood that it's not an option but a necessity to ensure the best outcome and desired results. When a dog is applauded for bringing the tennis ball back, it runs even faster the next time the ball is thrown. When an employee is appreciated for completing the task in time, he works with a new zeal for the next assignment. The motivation level of a student who is given a shining star on his notebook is higher than those who aren't appreciated. This helps us easily conclude that in order to get what we want; we must acknowledge the efforts of those around us.

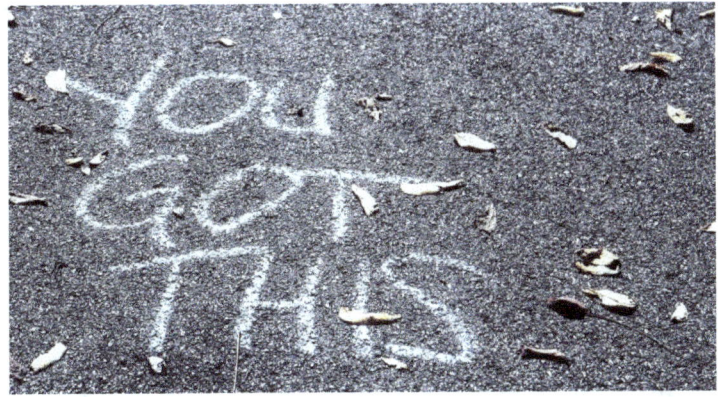

Asia Cup Final: 5 Runs needed on 1 ball, the batsman on strike is a bowler. The supporters cheer for them, the cricket stadium echoes with the national songs and you can feel the spirit in the air. The ball comes towards him, a Yorker, onto his feet. The batsman takes two steps forward, swings his bat and there it goes… The ball is in the air! Into the crowd. It's SIX!

Restoration of self-confidence is necessary to make you believe in your capabilities. In a world where challenges are abounding, it's easy for us to feel discouraged. Sometimes we really need to be encouraged when life seems like a failure. We need to be appreciated when we are de-motivated; we need to be given hope when we have lost our morale. We need to be reminded of who we are when we fail to accept ourselves. This is when encouragement is needed the most. Talking about someone who thinks he isn't worthy enough or he cannot win, something as effortless as a smile can motivate him to carry on. Let it be a national song or a motivational speech, smile from our parents or acknowledgment from our teachers, encouragement in every form is beneficial and healthy.

The benefits of encouragement include minimal chances of withdrawal because when we are ensured that it will be worth it in the end, we tend to get on with it. The words of encouragement work as energy pills, they ensure that there is light at the end of the tunnel. Challenges can make us physically and emotionally drained but the right words revitalize us. Encouragement, in other words, is empowerment, a confidence booster, and the healthiest motivator.

It is said that when a child comes into this world, his/her personality is as vulnerable and flexible as candle wax. During the first few years of his life, he/she can be molded into a different human being. Who tells him about the Quran or the Bible? Who defines the rights and wrongs? It's the parents, the molds, who shape his/her identity and define him into someone who is now adapted to survive in all conditions.

It can thus be said that parents have the most important impact on the life of a person. Their words can build up our confidence and at the same time shatter it too. Parents should be very picky about what they choose to say to their children. They must be careful because they are the ones who influence their children the most. As far as toddlers are concerned, the impact of encouragement on their life is indeed the greatest. Toddlers are not really aware of the rights and wrongs, perhaps, the rules of living in this world. This is where encouragement plays a role. Encouraging words can have a powerful impact on kids. This is because of positive reinforcement which encourages the child to repeat the praised behavior. Whether be it an academic achievement or the field of sports, encouraging words from elders can boost up the confidence of children.

Not all encouraging words carry the same weight. If used indiscriminately, some types of encouragement can cause more harm than good. The idea lies in the fact that "How" and "When" children are praised. There are numerous ways of appreciating your child: His actions can be applauded, a thumbs up or the sign of "Good Job!" can uplift his confidence. Different ways of encouragement have different impacts in varying situations.

When we say encouragement means motivation, by saying so, we mean that when children are appreciated, they tend to perform better. This is not only another impact of encouragement on children but also a driving force to ensure a better outcome. Taking the example of a toddler, when he is learning to walk and take his first steps if the parent moves to a distance and calls him, he tends to move towards his parent. The parent continues to appreciate the child by applauding his efforts and is advised to move back slowly, thus increasing the distance between him and the toddler. This form of encouragement says, "Good, you can do better" and thus, the toddler learns to walk over greater distances.

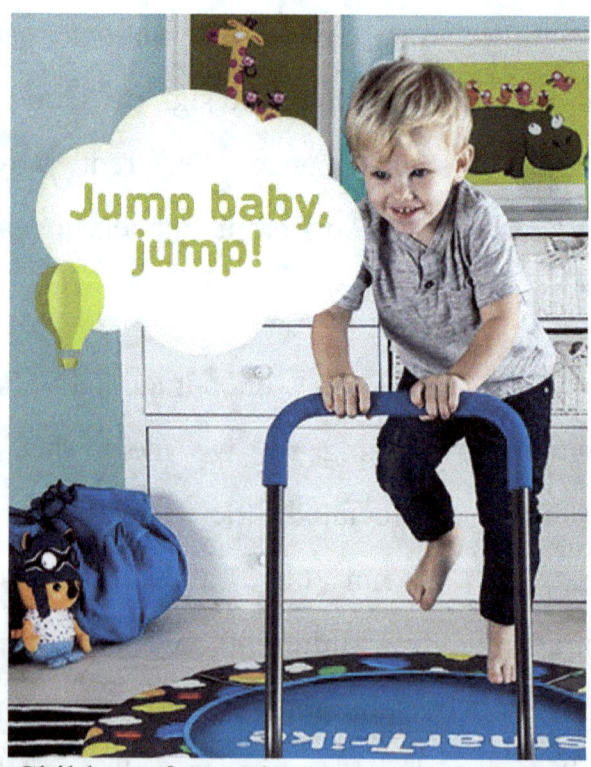

Children from the age of two years start developing a sense of self-worth. They start understanding different forms of appreciation and at the same time, they like to be valued. When a toddler notices that his elder sibling is being rewarded for doing something, he often repeats the task according to his own capabilities to seek the same appreciation. Similarly, young children are often very sensitive about their mothers, they like to be valued and encouraged all the time. The children who are thus, encouraged by their parents develop a positive self-worth. They adopt an attitude where they think they can do anything and they believe in themselves because when they were younger, their parents appreciated them enough to eliminate all the doubts they have in their capabilities.

On the contrary, the children who are often criticized by their parents unnecessarily develop negative self-worth that consequently leads to their failures in life. When a toddler is not appreciated for drawing a tree, then he will forever doubt his ability to do so. When a toddler is not applauded for taking his first shaky steps, he will always think he isn't good enough in taking steps towards anything. Unnecessary criticism is often done to seek perfection and parents think that correcting their children in almost everything will eliminate all flaws in them. However, it has a counter effect. Such children develop a feeling of not being good enough, even when their work is good according to their age. This makes them think that they are a failure. Parents should encourage their children to do better and better but there's always a proper way to say it out without them thinking that their work wasn't wonderful. Encouragement has a very important impact on the mind of a toddler.

It is easy to fall into the habit of praising by comparison. In almost all fields of life, humans are in competition. It has come to a level where even encouragement comes in comparison. However, this kind of comparison praise must be avoided for toddlers. They should always be encouraged on the basis of what they have achieved because, at times, it motivates them to work better. For example, two toddlers trying to sing a poem often competes with the other to sing louder and rhyme better. However, at times, it backfires. Considering Toddlers who are learning to take their first steps, when two of them are made to run side by side, one who is not able to maintain his balance as much as the other, tends to sit down and give up. This is why they must be appreciated by what they have achieved, not on how much more they have achieved than others. This is a very important point when it is about praising your child in the right way such that the encouragement has a positive impact on their young minds.

Children must be encouraged sincerely and honestly. Insincere praises are not only ineffective but also cause harm. They become accustomed to constant encouragement and appreciation to an extent that when they are not applauded, they underestimate their actions and start doubting their work, drowning in a feeling that makes them question their worth. In reality, their work is good but they just need someone to overestimate everything. Thus, this habit of requiring acknowledgment at every point of their lives makes children unsuccessful and fussy.

Similarly, easy tasks and over-praise must be avoided at every cost. Praising a toddler excessively for something insignificant makes him select easy tasks for the sake of appreciation from his parents and stops him from choosing something big. Frequent praising also makes them think that the absence of praise signifies failure.

Children must be encouraged using descriptive and specific comments instead of sweeping praises. Specific and descriptive comments show that you really paid attention to their work and that you care. Instead of appreciating a toddler by saying "Well done!" when he assembles the blocks in a shape of a house, acknowledge his efforts by telling him how colorful it is and that his choice of colors is captivating. This shows you sincerely paid attention to what he made and that makes him perform even better next time because he knows his parents will closely look into his new idea.

Children are more likely to repeat behavior that earns praise. This means praise can be used to help change difficult behavior and replace it with desirable behavior. When the desired behavior is seen, it should be praised. This develops a feeling of appreciation in the young mind of the toddler and hence, he is expected to repeat the desired behavior numerous times to seek the attention and the reward he is given. For example, if the toddler is learning to speak, the parent should reward him the toys only when he tries to use words. In this case, toys act as a reward. The toddler will try to use more and more words to convey his point and tell his parents that he wants the toys. Here, encouragement is a temptation which compels the toddler to do the desired actions. Encouragement can be done in different ways and always has a powerful impact on the mind of the toddler.

Sometimes, toddlers are encouraged in a way that they take it as a challenge. When we ask them to show us how fast they can run or let's see how well they can spell it. In this case, the parents are not only encouraging their children to do better but also motivating them to take difficult tasks as a challenge where the children think we must do it because then we will be appreciated.

A promising reward is also a common form of encouragement. It is needed to initiate something, to continue something or to stop doing something that causes damage. Tempting a toddler to crawl towards a bar of chocolate is encouragement, placing an object higher and expecting the toddler to maintain his balance and pick it up is both a challenge and encouragement.

Praise or encouragement is a double-sided sword. If parents use it wisely, being aware of the impacts of what they do and what they say on the minds of the toddlers, it can be a very powerful motivational force and learning tool.

CHAPTER SIX "SELF-EFFICACY & SELF-CONFIDENCE"

What is self-efficacy? Self-efficacy is your ability to solve a situation or in other words, your belief in your abilities to deal with the various situation. The concept of self-efficacy was proposed by a psychologist, Albert Bandura.

Some people work hard and strive for success, whereas on the other side, there are people that just let their life pass without any certain aims or perspectives. People tend to only try things; they will believe they will be successful. For example, you work at a store and they ask you to create a spreadsheet on the monthly sales. In your entire life, you have never created a spreadsheet. It doesn't mean that you should refuse the objective given, instead, you should strive and learn the spreadsheet to make a monthly sales report. If a person thinks that he is capable of accomplishing a task, the person will have a higher self-efficacy. On the other side, if the person thinks that he is not capable of accomplishing the given task, his self-efficacy level is low.

Similarly, children also have self-efficacy in themselves. The higher self-efficacy in children is linked to higher motivation, greater resilience, lower vulnerability to stress and depression, better ability to think productively by applying positive thinking skills when facing a challenge, and a stronger effort put into a certain task or activity. On the other hand, lower self-efficacy is linked with the tendency to shy away from difficult tasks, lower aspirations and poor commitment to goals, a pessimistic attitude towards obstacles, and greater vulnerability to stress and depression.

Self-efficacy is influenced by several factors:

- <u>Performance Accomplishments</u>: It means that how successful you have been in your past related to a specific task. Suppose, you have applied for a course to learn PowerPoint. If you had no difficulty in learning the course, you will feel more confident in performing a task in the future related to PowerPoint. This means that you will have higher efficacy for this type of task. On the other hand, if you had issues in learning the course, you will hesitate to work for that field. Therefore, your efficacy level will be lower in the related field to that course.

In the case of children, your child would be more confident if he had easily accomplished the task before. Or else, the child would fear to try to do the task again as he doesn't have trust in his abilities. This means that the child is lacking self-efficacy. Parents should always boost their children for trying new things and they should make sure that the child is happily engaged in the work. The first impression of anything on a children's brain will remain forever.

- <u>Vicarious Experiences</u>: It means to observe someone very similar to you. You will observe and implement the things in your life. For example, if your co-worker is working hard on a project and is trying to produce a great outcome, you will try to act similarly. Your efficacy level will increase and you will produce a very similar result. However, on the other hand, if the co-worker is struggling with a project and finding it hard to produce a result, your efficacy level will drop. You will also find it hard in that project.

In the case of children, they tend to follow their parents or their siblings. Sometimes we see children following the activities of their friends or siblings. If a random child is active in building a castle at a beach, your child will also build a castle with higher efficacy. This means that the child has boosted his efficacy by vicarious experiences.

- <u>Verbal Persuasion</u>: This is very similar to encouraging someone for a particular task. For example, if someone encourages you by saying, "You can do this.", the efficacy level will increase. However, on the other hand, if someone discourages you by saying, "This is too much for you.", the efficacy level will decrease and you will find it hard in completing that task.

The children are very sensitive to verbal persuasion. If you keep on discouraging your child, this will have a disastrous impact on the child's brain development and growth. The entire personality will be ruined. They won't be productive in any part of life and they would be scared of implanting new things. Moreover, they will not get curious about new learning activities. The discouragement would have a huge impact on their brain. It is therefore recommended to boost the courage and potential of your children by continuously motivating them and encouraging them. Most importantly, they would be more productive if they hair praise for their effort than their abilities.

- <u>Physiological States</u>: It depends on the emotional state, mood, anxiety level, etc. If you are healthy, your efficacy is higher. If you are feeling low or sick, your efficacy is lower.

  In the case of children, it is linked with their health. If the child is healthy and active, he will have greater efficacy than a child that is feeling lethargic and sick all the time. The parents should keep great care of their children's health. Make sure that the immune system of the children is fully active and healthy. A slight distraction can bring huge harm to your child. Apart from this, keep interacting with your children. This will help you understand their problems and make a stronger bond with them. Their physiological state will improve with your slight attention.

"Self-efficacious children tend to attribute their successes to ability, but ability attributions affect performance indirectly through perceived self-efficacy." –Albert Bandura.

What is self-confidence? It is the courage and ability to accept yourself or to believe in yourself. The definition is not sufficient itself, so let's give you an example. Suppose, you are working in an organization and you are a very hardworking employee. One day, your boss asks you to give a presentation to the buyers. The buyers are really important for the organization and the boss doesn't want to lose them. At this point, you have immense responsibility and pressure on your shoulders. Many of the people lose their skills, courage, abilities, and potential at this point. They lose their self-confidence and shiver with fear and anxiety. If you have self-confidence, you will have believed in yourself and your skills. You would have shown a greater outcome than an average employee. Self-confidence provides the courage and ability to get your point of view approved. If you have self-confidence, you can achieve your goals.

Look around at those politicians, they dare to get their words approved in the assembly. From where do they get this potential and courage? It is all from self-confidence. To stand against the opposition, one must believe in oneself. If they don't believe in themselves, everyone will ignore their point of view. They will not be considered an important part of the assembly. To be self-confident means, you are believing the points you are presenting and perusing people to follow it. Many of the great influencers, presenters, and speakers have self-confident. They know the way to keep their audience attracted to themselves. This is their skill and they have trust in their mastery. For a greater example, refer to the motivational speakers. Look at the way they keep themselves attached to the audience. In no time, they create a bond with the viewers. Instead of fearing the reactions and views of the people, they stand firm and deliver their thought with a great strategy. The strategy is nothing, but self-confidence. Self-confidence is generated and build with experience.

Self-confidence is influenced by the following factors. The following factors are linked with the development of parent's self-confidence.

The child learns from their parents and the parents must develop self-confidence in themselves.

- <u>Identify your negative thoughts</u>: Your negative thought creates a hindrance in your path to success. As we have learned in the belief system, the negative thoughts are created by the conscious mind and it has a negative effect on the subconscious mind. These negative thoughts can be controlled by our self. It just requires some motivation and uplifting. To boost and build your self-confidence, one must identify its negative thoughts and convert them into positive ones. Think more positive than negative, give positive thoughts more space in your brain than negative thoughts. The subconscious mind is like a warehouse and filling it up with positivity will boost your self-confidence. Avoid spending time around things that make you feel bad or lower your self-confidence.

Take out some time from your busy routine and mark the things that disturb your peaceful mind. Filter them out and you will observe the happiness in your life.

- <u>Maintain a positive support network</u>: If people keep on discouraging you, you will have low self-confidence. Your social pressure and fear will increase and you will not be able to interact much with the outer world. Let's take an example, you are a child whose parents keeps on discouraging their child by saying that the child is not capable and is weak. Even though if the child is all good and perfect, he will feel sad and will have lower self-confidence. This is just a small example related to motivation. If someone motivates you, you perform better. However, if someone continuously disturbs you and discourage you, the person will think negative of himself and will remain in depression. It is recommended to keep a positive support network. Stay in people that help you in your difficult time and stand beside you whenever you need any help. *"A person is known by the company he keeps."*

- <u>Identify your talents and make a productive lifestyle:</u> Keep yourself involved in your habits and interests. Permit yourself in taking pride in them. Express yourself through different hidden talents of yours. You will feel unique and accomplished. There is a greater chance that you will find a compatible friend in your field of interest. Believe in yourself and start taking pride in yourself.

For example, if a person loves singing and music, he will keep himself involved in the activities in his free time. He will have no time to think about the negativity around him. Interestingly, he can earn from his interests. This will make him more confident and will make him more relaxed in a hectic life. Moreover, accept the compliments gracefully. If you have a lower level of self-confidence, you will find it hard to accept a compliment from somebody. You will think that the person is either lying or mistaken.

- <u>Stop comparing yourself with others</u>: This is the biggest hindrance in the path to self-confidence. In this world, nobody is equal. Everyone has its potential, stamina, thinking, capabilities, strategies, etc. Don't make your life as your best friend's life. Think differently and make life as you desire than the desire of the people around you. Try to stand aside from the crowd as it requires self-confidence to be different. Let's take a brief example, if a child's parents are constantly comparing their child with some other child, there is a chance that the child will follow the other child than perusing his dreams. The child will go against his subconscious mind and will get weaker with time. His self-confidence will shatter with time. Always keep a card that is different from others, this will make you special in society and will increase your self-confidence.

Stop Comparing Your Writing Harshly With Other People's Work

- <u>Learn from your mistakes</u>: This is the most important tip in boosting your self-confidence. The ego destroys the personality of the people. Don't let your inner ego destroy your impression in others' eyes. If you work on your mistake, you will excel in your life. Don't lose hope by failing at one time. Keep on trying and trying until to succeed in your task. If you don't learn from your mistakes, how will you learn to improve? Think for a minute, is it possible to achieve something without even trying for it? No! This is not how things work. You have to put an effort into the tasks you do. If you learn from your mistakes, you will grow more confident. You will be able to express and face people with more confidence. There is a great chance that you will learn something unique while improving your mistakes. In this way, your extra knowledge will increase. People will appreciate you for your knowledge and wisdom. Learning from mistakes is the golden key to boost self-confidence.

CHAPTER SEVEN "INTERESTS & HOBBIES"

What is an interest or a hobby? An interest or a hobby is an activity that a person enjoys. It helps them understand what they really like doing and are good at. Interest and hobby can be a path for them to help them realize what they enjoy doing in their free time and how they can help themselves with these skills when they learn to do something in their normal daily chores. When a toddler is determined to carry up a hobby, he or she will first eventually fail at it or find it difficult but if they really like doing the thing or eventually want to get better at it, they will learn how to do things the hard way rather than giving up.

The hobbies and interests which a person develops are of different types and of different nature. The hobbies can be either indoor, outdoor, related to nature, sports, intellectual and fitness, etc.

The main point is that the parents must help their children to think out of the box and develop extracurricular activities. The parents must help their child in keeping it fun and not obsessing over it. Some parents, for example, make it very hard for their child to enjoy a certain hobby by putting in a lot of pressure.

Sports. This one word carries in it a wide variety of hobbies. The sports are further divided into indoor and outdoor sports. Some children prefer to go outside in the dirt and play it rough while others have fun in more sophisticated forms of indoor sports. Some parents make a poor choice when they tell their children they can't do one thing or another based on gender discrimination or the fact that playing indoor makes them feminine. The parents must not make this a competition between children and try to make their kid stronger and better than that of their friend, family or neighbor. Hobbies of children are not something to be made a competition out of but of course, healthy competition is always good. For that purpose, if your child enjoys sports, you must have him signed up for sports clubs where they can explore and learn about their hobbies and interests from elders and interact with people with the same interests. They are also more likely to make new friends like this and health is always a side benefit when it comes to sports.

    Joining a sports club will also help your child understand the importance of sportsmanship. He will make new friends and eventually rule out the part where your child is often isolated and ends being bullied for not having any friends. They will have people around them who share the same interest and enjoy the company of each other. Sports like cricket, football, soccer, squash, badminton, basketball, hockey, tennis, table tennis, golf, skating, baseball, cycling, running, volleyball, swimming can really help your child utilize his free time in something useful and eventually learn a new set of skills.

Music for some people is an art. An art for relaxation and expressing your inner true feelings. It is considered one of the very best hobbies to make your mind sharp either by writing a song or learning how to play different pieces of musical equipment. If your child wants to learn how to play the guitar or the piano or even drums, you must totally help them learn that by teaching it yourself or hiring for them a tutor to do so. In this manner, your child will be able to play what he likes. First, they will start playing in front of friends, then their family and eventually they will muster up enough courage to go on stage for school or any other event. Thus, they will be quite confident to help them in their lives ahead of them. This can also serve as a means for the family can get together to have a karaoke session and spend some quality time together.

On the other hand, the hobbies which really help you boost your brainpower are board games. They are a good opportunity for the family to sit together and play board games together. Cards and board games help make the mind sharp. Examples of these games are chess, scrabble, monopoly, Uno, etc. Chess is an apt game for the development of mental skills and is very competitive at the same time. It helps the children learn to play by the rules and think a lot before making any move thus, helping in the development of making decisions and being careful with every step of their lives. In addition to this, scrabble is a useful game to help children learn new words to increase their vocabulary and help improve their English for school. Therefore, board games in general without bets are a good activity for children in their extra time as they directly help in the sharpening of the mind.Another hobby which a lot of children surprisingly like and is generally loved by parents more often is reading. Many children pick up the habit of reading novels and comics and everything of this sort. Reading books and comics directly gives them new ideas and makes their minds sharper and more intellectual. Reading varying viewpoints of different writers and authors helps them think more vastly about a certain perspective. Some children, on the other hand, like to listen to stories. Mystery, comedy, drama, etc. are good choices available to the children. However, parents should be extra careful to read the books themselves first to make sure there is no element of violence or crime which the child can pick out of it. There are special programs carried out in many libraries where a group of kids who share the love for books are gathered in a certain time period and are allowed to explore the libraries for the books they like to read in the kids' section. Here, they sit down together for a reading program where an elder reads the book out loud to them and lets them question to which he/she provides answers queries related to the book, thereby, leading to a better understanding.

Some children, at a very tender age, like, to earn money even if they have little or no concept about it. It can be either very useful or very detrimental to one's mind if they cultivate the mindset where they give a lot of value to monetary things. An apt example is where children set up garage sales for their old toys and make lemonade stalls in the neighborhood. This instills in them a sense of working and obviously helps them learn skills like bargaining. It also makes them learn that they must let things go once they are not in their use.

Some children have a very interesting and mechanical mind where they tend to break the toys they get and then try to join them together into an object completely different from the original one. This really helps them learn creativity and think outside the box. As an example, when children break down their remote-control cars to make a fan out of the motor and make a cart out of the wheels, avoid stopping them from doing such practices as the result will only be productive in letting them think of something clever and creative. Allow them to explore things and go on wild adventures by themselves but always make sure that whatever they are doing is totally safe by making them learn precautionary measures.

Some children like to play outside in the dirt and mud. Building sandcastles, mud houses, small irrigation systems in their gardens is what the kids can do to learn a different set of skills on how the things around them are made. The next time they see a huge tower they will question you on how it was made and you must encourage them to make one for themselves by playing in the mud and with sand. Another good exercise for building towers is Legos and puzzles.

Another interest which the children develop is keeping pets. Whether that be a dog, a cat, a fish, a bird or any other pet for that matter, the parents generally disagree with them. The matter of fact is that it can be a good exercise for them to learn how to take care of something and be dutiful towards something they are responsible for taking care of. Children normally fall in love with their pets and do everything it takes to take full care of them. Thus, it gives them a sense of responsibility to feed their pet, to play with their pet, to bathe them, to take them out for a walk and to give them water and snacks at the right time of the day in the right amount.

On the other hand, some children enjoy doing gaming. This carries its own advantages and disadvantages. The advantage is that it brings out new abilities related to learning about technology and software. However, on the other hand, the disadvantage is that it can be highly addictive often resulting in bad grades of the students. Video games can lead to a very detrimental impact on health if not taken care of in time. Games often include violence and killing which is embedded in the child's mind as fun. Sitting in front of a couch for long hours without any physical activity and interaction with the outside world may lead to obesity and can also be a cause of your child becoming devoid of a social circle. Thus, the use of video games should be kept to a certain extent with strictly observed playing hours.

Some children like to watch cartoons and baby tv on their television, laptop, iPad or tablets. This, in a similar manner, can be of advantage where they learn the alphabets, counting, and shapes but at the same time, excessive watching can lead to addiction after which even mundane actions like eating or drinking their milk, will be affected badly until their favorite cartoons aren't played.

Some kids find it amusing to make videos, especially, in this century where YouTube is very common in every household. Little children like to make videos about toy reviews and other things about them completing a task and uploading it for the world to see can be very interesting. This medium serves more advantages than disadvantages.

Children who have a love for nature love gardening. Together with their parents, they plant flowers and other plants and make sure to water them daily. This is very beneficial as it inculcates in them a sense of responsibility as to water the plants on time and while doing so, they will love the outdoor and fresh air while admiring the aesthetics of nature at the same time.

The love for art is a very deep love indeed. Children love to paint and make drawings which is a good means of expressing their inner emotions. The parents must encourage them to pursue this forward and ask them the idea behind their drawing. Upon asking, one will be surprised to find out what goes on in the mind of a child. Parents must always encourage them with appreciative words about their drawings and often take them to exhibits to imbibe more.

Collecting items is something a lot of children are fond of. Whether that be the caps of bottles or coins, it gives the children a good idea of how to work hard for something with patience. One will notice the fact that children tend to research things they like to collect thus, always leading to an increase in their general knowledge. Children also love dramas and shows. You must encourage your child to be a part of school dramas and plays to help boost their self-morale and confidence.

Children often have a love for food. They sit around in the kitchen and help their parents in cooking which leads to them learning as well as spending quality time with their family. Going to the gym with parents or fishing with fathers and being interested in gymnastics and martial arts or karate are all activities that can lead to great skill development in your child.

Thus, hobbies and interests are quite productive unless the parents or children make it an obsession and lose sleep over it. They are always beneficial when kept fun.

CONCLUSION

In light of the evidence mentioned above, it can be concluded that the baby's brain is very sensitive from the beginning to the age of five years. The parents need to take special care of their children in this age period. The baby's brain tends to develop neurons and build up cognitive abilities and potential in this period. Apart from this, the baby's learning potential is highest at this stage or time.

In the first chapter, the book mentions ways to stimulate the baby's brain. It also discusses the effects of stimulating the baby's brain on productivity and abilities. In the second chapter, the book talks about parenting tips and the ways to improve the relationship/bond between parents and children.

In the third chapter, the book discusses the benefits of mindfulness and gratitude. It mentions how the topic affects the brain development of a child. The mindfulness and gratitude will enhance the personality of the child in the long-run. The fourth chapter is about the diet of a toddler. For sure, the diet has a great impact on the cognitive development of the child. If you are providing quality food and great nutrition, your child will have a greater IQ and potential.

In the fifth chapter, the book provides information to the parents about the encouragement and its effects on the child's brain development. Encouragement is very motivational for children and is a driving force for future successes. The sixth chapter targets self-confidence and self-efficacy. The book trains the parents by providing them tips to enhance their self-confidence as children tend to learn from their parents. It also marks some factors that help the child in boosting his self-efficacy.

Lastly, the seventh chapter is about promoting the interest and hobbies of a child.

Promoting will help the child to build more confidence and become more creative. It will enhance his working potential and abilities. This book is a comprehensive guide for parents to help their child in brain development in early ages.

PART 2

A COMPLETE GUIDE TO ENCOURAGING CHILDREN EXPRESS THEIR EMOTIONS AND UNDERSTAND THEIR FEELINGS TO FEEL CALM AND FOCUSED ANYTIME

CONTENTS

DESCRIPTION 124

INTRODUCTION 129

CHAPTER ONE "TEACHING GRATITUDE" 134

CHAPTER TWO "TEACHING MINDFULNESS" 157

CHAPTER THREE "EXPRESSING THEIR THOUGHTS" 169

CHAPTER FOUR "SELF-CONFIDENCE" 178

CONCLUSION 193

DESCRIPTION

The book is a complete guide for teachers and parents to teach their children about the developing creativeness in the world. Children themselves can read the book to become encouraged about the mindfulness and cognitive abilities. They will realize the need for becoming more thoughtful and confident to stand in the competitive world. In today's world, the grades are not considered much compared to the creativeness and skillfulness. The book will touch every perspective of this category and will show the outcome for every perspective.

Apart from this, the book deals with the teaching of expressing yourself through words. If you can't stand or represent yourself, you have no chance of success in this world. The book gives a detailed tips and tricks of how to express yourself. It also mentions some examples, quoted from real life, to make you more interested in the topic. Examples can be a good source to encourage someone for a particular task or thing.

Furthermore, the book provides the significance of showing gratitude. It tells the reader about the ways of developing the nature of appreciation in oneself and the changes it can make in your life. Teaching kids the art of gratitude will make them prosper in their future life. In this category, the book quotes some examples from famous personalities to encourage the reader for practicing gratitude. Other than this, the book mentions some strategies to make yourself more appreciative. The strategies will include some random examples to provide better understanding and purpose of the strategy.

In the end, the book discusses about the necessity of confidence. It gives some tips and tricks to develop confidence for a better and successful life. The book also provides an authentic source to the reader, a study, about the confidence and its impact on life. It is indeed a fact that majority of the population lacks confidence. Just look around yourself, you will see many people losing their rights and conversation to other people. Many people are forced to remain quiet and are suppressed by the dominants. Many people don't take actions against the administration, they continue suffering from the strict policies and non-humanitarian working principals. What are they all lacking? They all are lacking confidence. They don't have the courage to stand for their rights and express themselves. Therefore, from the very beginning children should be taught of how to stand strong and face the situations of the world.

All the things mentioned in the book have some impact on your personality, so it is recommended to give a read with full concentration and will. For sure, after reading this book, you will feel the urge to bring the change in your personality. Let's jump into it and extract the knowledge for better and healthy future.

INTRODUCTION

There is a constant effort in making this world a better place for living. The people are thinking out of the box to produce things that are hard to imagine. In just twenty to thirty years, the world had gone through vast changes and these changes are unstoppable. Who are these people that are bringing changes in this world? They are no different than us; all of them are humans. They have the ability to use their creativeness to produce things that are not understandable by most of the people around us. They know the power of their brain and their skills, and they know the right way to implement it.

It is getting very necessary to teach our children for becoming more and more mindful, so they can also think out of the box in complicated or complex situations. Mostly, the children prefer staying in a cozy environment and doesn't want to explore their hidden abilities. They are either scared or not motived enough to step outside. There are many other factors that can be a hindrance in growing, e.g. confidence, self-efficacy, social pressure, etc.

In this growing world, everyone wants to be a part of the establishment and be an active member of the society. To be amongst the representative, people are standing and raising their voice. The representation scenario is everywhere; in your classroom, in your student council committee, in the parliaments, etc. If you are unable to represent yourself, you stand nowhere and everyone will consider you as weak and in minorities. If you want to grow and have a successful future, it is extremely important to learn the skill of representing yourself. Make sure that people don't take you for granted and should understand your importance. All this is possible if you keep a good track of your personality, confidence, and being more active in the world around you.

"It is only with gratitude that life becomes rich!" -Dietrich Bonhoeffer.

The above quotation has a very deep meaning. It tells the reader that be thankful for whatever you have and this appreciation will make you feel rich. The humans can't be satisfied with whatever they have. We will constantly work hard to achieve our dreams. Even after our dreams are achieved, we will start working on some other wish. This makes gives us more stress and tension. If we practice gratitude and make it part of our life, we will never have tensions and stress. All these diseases and aging would vanish away. We will be more relaxed than ever. All we have to do is to practice gratitude and bring it in our life. We should teach our children to practice gratitude from the very beginning, so they don't suffer later in life.

"Do the difficult things while they are easy and do the great things while they are small. A journey of a thousand miles must begin with a single step." - Lao Tzu.

Considering the quote of the philosopher, we will begin our journey to bring changes in ourselves and our children.

CHAPTER ONE "TEACHING GRATITUDE"

Before starting the chapter and get into its specifications, we need to know the meaning of the term, gratitude. What is Gratitude? Gratitude means to be thankful for whatever you have or be appreciative and return kindness. It's a quality that everyone should have in them. Gratitude is a feeling of being rich and better in every situation.

Mostly in class, children are trying their best to be better than the other student. They will try to copy them and will do anything to be above them. Here, the children are lacking gratitude as they are not happy for what they have. For example, a child in a class brings an IPhone and the other child brings a handset that it not up to that IPhone standard. Now, the child without an IPhone will feel lower than the child having an IPhone because he is not happy for what he has. He will constantly thing of himself as lower than him and this will make him unhappy and stressful.

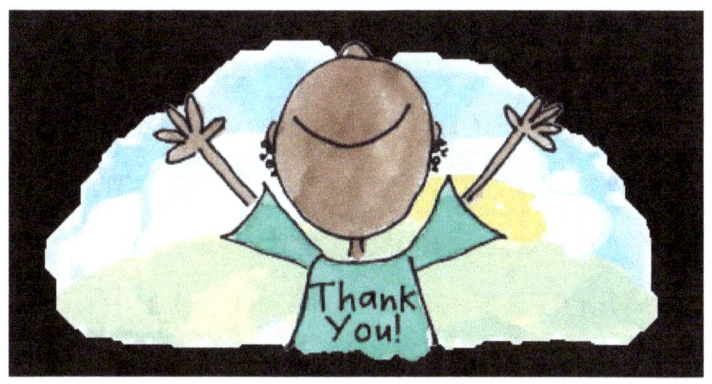

If a child has gratitude, he will be grateful for whatever he has. He will never judge people and will ignore the materialistic society. A person can't be mature enough until he has gratitude in himself. There are numerous advantages a child can gain by practicing gratitude. Some of the advantages are listed below:

- **MORE FRIENDS AND FOLLOWINGS**: Having gratitude means that you are filled with a lot of positivity. You have no room for negativity and prefers to stay happy all the time. You appreciate everything, including your friends. You will give them respect and will thank them for whatever they do for you. Having gratitude means that you are loyal and don't betray people around you. In today's world, loyalty is rarely seen. This quality of yours will encourage other people to become friends with you. They will also try to follow your footsteps due to your quality of appreciation.

For example, a stranger is holding a door for you and you thank him for his respectful behavior. This will create a sense of relationship between you both and a beginning of friendship. The stranger will have a positive image of yours and would love to interact with you (Positivity attract others!). Therefore, having gratitude and kindness will bring you more friends and followings. You will never get bored again with lots of friends.

- **<u>BETTER PHYSICAL HEALTH</u>**: This is the most important advantage for having gratitude in your personality. Nothing is more important than a better health. A study had shown that having gratitude reduces the aches and pains in the body.

How does body health relate with gratitude? Gratitude is a quality of being thankful for whatever you have. It means that we don't have to stress ourselves to work for extra hours for better grades or pay. If you don't take stress, you have a better health and calm mind. The chaos is the major reason for diseases and mind frustration.

For example: A person is working as a security guard in an organization. He stands and lifts heavy weight of the gun for eight hours to earn money for his living. If the guard has gratitude, he will be satisfied with his life and would try to adjust in his earning. However, on the other hand, the guard will continue working in shifts (extra hours) to earn more, for his satisfaction, if he has no gratitude or sense of appreciation (He will never get satisfied and will spend rest of his life working and working). Working extra hours without giving required break to your body and brain will cause pain and physical health misbalance. Always be thankful for what you have and ignore the greed for more. This will increase your life expectancy and your life will become healthier than ever. It is very necessary to teach your child gratitude, so they don't suffer from deteriorating health in their early age.

- **IMPROVES PSYCHOLOGICAL HEALTH:** Gratitude reduces a multitude of toxic emotions, ranging from envy and resentment to frustration and regret. Robert A. Emmons, Ph.D., a leading gratitude researcher, has conducted multiple studies on the link between gratitude and well-being. His research confirms that gratitude effectively increases happiness and reduces depression.

When you are happy with your life, there is nothing that can ruin your mood or make you stressful. You will have a positive nature in the society and people will appreciate you and your presence. Hormones are severely affected by our mood, so having a positive routine and life will keep your hormones balanced. You won't have toxicity in your life and your life would be great. You will have a better relationship, a happy family, and a happy job. There won't be anything that can be the cause for frustration resentment or regret.

In case of children, their behavior would be perfect and they won't react to the situations around them. They will absorb everything calmly and will grow in a perfect way possible. They will have no disturbance and therefore, no depression. Many students are taking pressure for studies and grades. This can be reduced if children practice gratitude and appreciate themselves for the effort they put into exams.

- **REDUCES AGGRESSION:** Many parents complain about their children becoming more and more aggressive. There are many factors that contributes to their aggression. The biggest and most significant factor is lack of gratitude. If the children appreciate and accept their blessings, they will never show aggression and stress. Children should be taught that they should accept and stay happy with the things they have. This will make them understand their responsibilities and they will come out of their fake dreams. Try showing them the reality, so they should understand and interpret the true world. Practicing gratitude will surely reduce the anger and aggression in the children. They will become kindhearted and will have bigger heart for everyone.

For example: A child believes that he should have a new phone just like his friend. He will talk to his parents, but they don't allow him to have one at the moment. The child will continue persuading his parents for getting him a new phone until he becomes frustrated and starts showing aggression. To prevent this, the child should learn gratitude. He should understand that parents don't think bad for their children and at the moment, they are not able to give him a phone. The child should learn to stay happy with current phone.

The gratitude will make the child's heart as open as an ocean. He will understand and accept other people and their perspective. He will appreciate people with their nature and behavior instead of materialistic things. The child will show no aggression and will be stress free. There will be no depression nor anxiety in the child.

- **<u>BETTER SLEEP AND INCREASED MENTAL STRENGTH</u>**: Of course when you are happy with whatever you have, there will be no room for stress, over-thinking, anxiety, money pressure, etc. This will allow the person to have restful nights and sweet dreams. Gratitude has a direct effect on your cognitive abilities.

"There is a calmness to a life lived in gratitude, a quite joy."

The above quote expresses the importance of gratitude on life. Let there be peace with gratitude. Sleeping more than eight hours a day is a surety to better health and healthy heart. It is said that most of the diseases starts with stress and anxiety. It is recommended to practice gratitude as it will keep you safe from majority of the diseases. Your mind will relax and will be pressure free. You can use your brain to produce other creative products or contents. This can increase your productivity and thus a better future.

Looking at the advantages we can conclude that practicing gratitude had great effect in our life, especially on our health. Gratitude is a quality that can change the fate of a person in no time. Gratitude can make you feel amongst the highest when you are feeling low. To make your life more relaxing and peaceful, one must practice gratitude. The following points will discuss tips and tricks for teaching children the art of gratitude.

- **SAY GRACE BEFORE EVERY MEAL:** In today's world, poverty is at extreme. People are unemployed and are unable to earn enough money to manage their needs. At every corner of the street, there are beggars fighting their situations.

Children are homeless and women are striving for shelters. In such situation, having a peaceful meal, three times a day, is a blessing. Children should be taught that they should say grace before every meal. This will bring gratitude in their nature and gratitude habituated through practice takes residence in the soul.

The children would also realize the value of food and will stop wasting it. Whenever we order something at the restaurants, a lot of food is wasted and goes to the garbage. It doesn't mean that we should stop going to the restaurants, rather we should give away that food to needy and homeless people. This will bring self-satisfaction and happiness to you and your children. In long run, these habits will shape the personality of your children.

- **EXPOSE THEM TO REALITY:** This is a really powerful technique to encourage your child for practicing gratitude. The media is nothing, but a disguise. The children should be taken outside in the real world to explore and interact. Show them the people that are not able to live lavishly or are homeless. Show them a storm-ravaged area or poverty-stricken area. Surely, showing is more powerful than telling.

The children will relate themselves to the situation they'll see. They will understand that world is not equal for everyone and that they should be grateful for whatever they have. They are living far better than most of the people!

Your child will ask you many questions and will learn from them, so it is better to be prepared when taking your child to a storm struck area or a community shelter. Interestingly, your child will encourage other children to visit those areas. This will increase awareness and gratitude in other children too and will have a long run benefit in the child's personality.

- **BE GRATEFUL PARENTS**: Your child is reflecting you! This is because they learn from you 24/7. The child won't be grateful if the parents or teachers are not grateful. Try bringing a positivity and sense of appreciation in the house or school for children to follow. Be grateful for your relationship, be grateful for your job and house, be grateful for food, be grateful for your lifestyle, be grateful for the things you have; these things will add up and form the nature and behavior of your child.

The children will implement the things in future that are done by their parents, so it is recommended to have a positivity around the child. Solve your matters alone or somewhere that doesn't affect your child's personality. The people will appreciate the child and indirectly, that appreciation is for the parents and the teachers for better grooming of the child. Let your child set examples for other children and to make you proud in the society or community.

Be Grateful Parents!

- **MAKE THEM EARN STUFF**: The simplest way to encourage your children for practicing gratitude is make them earn for their stuff. To be honest, this method will make them understand the value of money and effort. The children will appreciate their parent's effort and will thank them for whatever they have done for them. They will learn to invest the money properly and will not waste them. They will hold their unnecessary demands and will help their parents in every way possible. The children will understand the situation of other fellow students and will support them whenever they need some help. Most importantly, they will feel independent as they don't have to run behind anybody for their needs. They will feel mature and grown up. There are many ways for children to earn money:

- Clearing snow from the neighbor's porch or backyard.
- Taking neighbor's pet on walk
- Babysitting
- Food Stalls
- Selling old items, etc.

- **<u>MAKE SURE THEY SOMETIMES DON'T GET WHAT THEY WANT:</u>**

This may sound harsh, but this is also an important step in practicing gratitude. If you keep on giving away things to your children they desire, they might stop realizing the worth of it. They will never be able to learn gratitude.

For example: A child wants a Toy and the child's parents get him one. After two days, the child asks for another toy and the parents get him another one. Again, after two days, the child asks for another toy and the parents get him another toy again. What is happening here? The child is not realizing the worth of your money and toys.

Suppose that the next time child asks for the toy and the parents don't have the money to afford it. At this point, the child will start misbehaving and will become stubborn. He won't appreciate their parent's effort for previous toys, instead he will destroy them. The child won't be happy with the current toys and will continue asking for more. It would be difficult to get that nature out of the child, so it is recommended to not fulfil every desire of your child and start teaching them gratitude from the very beginning.

- **TEACH THEM TO SERVE OTHERS & BE GENEROUS:** Teach your children to give away their items to poor, needy, and homeless. This will encourage to serve the humanity. Generosity doesn't mean to give away any item or belonging, it means giving on a sacrificial level. Give away something that they love the most.

Real generosity is a huge step towards gratitude.

- **NEVER BAIL THEM OUT OF RESPONSIBILITIES**: Let them face the consequences of their action or decision, so they understand the difference between right and wrong. In this way, they will learn the reason for gratitude. Don't spoil them by giving away whatever they desire, instead share some responsibility to help them grow in the world. If we think that the lessons are too hard, they will never fully understand. This would have a long run effect on your child's nature, behavior, and personality.

"Gratitude creates the most wonderful feeling. It can resolve disputes. It can strengthen friendships. And, it makes us better men and women." –Gordon B. Hinckley.

CHAPTER TWO "TEACHING MINDFULNESS"

In the previous chapter, we have discussed about the ways for teaching children the quality of gratitude. In this chapter, we will learn about the methods, tips, and tricks for teaching our children the art of mindfulness. The chapter had immense importance in children's life.

What is mindfulness? It means to be aware of our feelings, thoughts, bodily sensation, and surrounding environments. In another foam, the state of knowing about something. In today's world, the mindfulness is rarely seen in people. Mindfulness reduces anxiety, depression, stress, eating disorders, and sleeping disorders. Mindfulness disentangles you from reacting to particular emotions and thoughts as you become a non-judgmental observer of yourself.

Mindfulness can be practiced in many different ways, e.g. meditations, physical practices, mindful eating, etc. It is necessary to teach your kids the skill of mindfulness. It will make them more relaxing, appreciative, and positive. The mindfulness is a quality that can help them succeed in the workplace as well as relationships.

There is an emerging body of research that indicates that mindfulness can help our children improve their abilities to pay attention, to calm down when they are upset, and to make better decisions. In short, with emotional regulation and cognitive focus.

The following bullets will help you teach your children the art of mindfulness.

- **<u>ESTABLISH YOUR OWN PRATICE</u>**: This is something that is necessary before you begin teaching your child about the art of mindfulness. You need to practice is yourself before teaching your child about mindfulness. In this way, you will be able to understand the right way to start the teaching process and the difficult steps in between. You will already have the idea of how to cope with the difficult steps and how to remain consistent throughout the practice duration. This will help you and your child in having a successful practice.

- **KEEP IT SIMPLE**: Don't stress it out on your children. Try keeping it low and easy for them to digest it. Make sure that the children like the practice idea. Introduce them new games that links with the mindful practice.

For example: you can ask your children to stay focused and listen to the sound played by you. The sound could be of a bell, a set of chimes, or a phone app that produces sound. They have to listen to the sound until it is over. This has a calm effect on the children and a fun way to teach them to pay attention to their surroundings.

- **CREATE A MINDFUL BEDTIME RITUAL:** Practicing mindfulness at night has the most effect on your child's nature and behavior. Night time has the maximum effect. There are many ways to help your child in learning the art of mindfulness. The following points give you the ways to help your child in practicing mindfulness at night or before bed:
  - **Short Body-Scan:** Tell your child to close their eyes and sense their body parts one by one. This will help them to get more focused, more relaxed, and more relieved. A calm way to return to the body at the end of the day.

- **Short Stories:** Tuck your child inside the bed and tell them a story that links with mindfulness. Tell them to stay relaxed and imagine the story in their mind. This will help them to absorb most of the story and store it in the brain. Short stories are a great way to deliver something to your child.
- **Thanks:** Try gratitude, it is the best way to practice mindfulness. Every night before bed, praise for whatever you have. Be thankful for the food, restful nights, home, family, toys, etc. Gratitude has many other great benefits and it helps

to shape your personality and nature.

- **PRACTICE WITH BREATHING BUDDIES**: One of the ways for children to focus better and strengthen their attention skills, particularly for concentration in school, is practicing with breathing buddies. Look around yourself, there are many children living in concentrated places with little to no peace. Honks, noise, pollution, etc. are part of their frustrated lives. It is very difficult for children from such places to concentrate and focus in the class or tasks.

However, there is a way to tackle this problem. The method is called breathing buddies. Ask your child to bring his small favorite stuff toy. Find a place to lie down, then put the stuff toy on their tummy and watch the breath go up and down. As the child breath in, count till three and then release. Repeat this procedure for five minutes. This is the self-management training and a great way to practice focus and mindfulness.

- **MINDFUL EATING GAME**: This is also the best way to practice mindfulness. Ask your child to stand at the door of the kitchen and sense the aroma of the food. Let them focus on the aroma and judge the menu for dinner, breakfast, or lunch.

Another way is to teach them to eat slowly. Give a break of twenty to thirty second between each bite to notice the taste and flavor of the food. If they are holding utensils, ask them to put it down until they finish chewing and swallowing. This is a great way to enhance the concentration and focus of the child.

Eating slowly has many other health advantages, e.g. the child will have a better stomach heath, absorption of food will be greater as the food will be better chewed, no bloating or nauseating feeling.

- **MINDFUL WALKING:** Tell you child that they can practice mindfulness even when they are in motion. They can sense the ground under their feet and can feel the movement of the body. They can feel the breeze moving through the hair or the clothes moving against the skin. Try focusing on breath when walking. This will help them to walk more and built greater stamina. They can even run a larger distance if they practice mindfulness.

Let your child excel in the world by practicing the art of mindfulness. Stay concentrated on the current situation and forget the unnecessary thoughts from your mind. Mindfulness is a great way to bring peace and happiness in your life.

"Do not dwell in the past, do not dream of the future, concentrate the mind on the present moment."

CHAPTER THREE "EXPRESSING THEIR THOUGHTS"

In the previous chapter, we have discussed about the ways of teaching the children about mindfulness. In this chapter, we will teach the children about expressing their thoughts. Of course, it is very difficult to survive in a world where you can't express yourself. Expressing yourself mean that you are able to deliver your thoughts, emotions, feelings, and ideas to another person or a group of people.

If a child is unable to express himself in a class, he will feel discouraged, low, and stressed. Everyone will make fun of him and consider him as a coward. Nobody wants to go through that experience! To become popular and active in a class, a child must master the skill of expressing himself. He should know the way to keep control of his emotions, expressions, thoughts and use it at the right time to leave an impression on the fellow classmates or teachers.

Nowadays, children are not being themselves. They are under peer pressure and media messages that tells them to obey if they want to become more popular and famous. To be part of a society, group, or a community, children are sacrificing their personal interests and tastes. This is killing the creativity and mindfulness in the children.

Teaching and encouraging the children for expressing their thoughts has immense benefits. Some of them are mentioned below:

Be emphatic and supportive

Perform better in school and carrer

Have positive and stable relationship

Feeling competent and confident,

There are many ways that encourages the children to express their thoughts. The following list mentions some of the most significant factors:

- **<u>TEACH KIDS TO EXPRESS THEMSELVES IN THE ART</u>**: This is a fun activity for the children and a great way to hear to their thoughts. Just give your child a blank paper and some color pencils, and wait for the result. You can use different music, dance, theater, crafts, etc. to encourage your child to express himself. For sure, every kid is unique and had different qualities. Keep on motivating them by cheering them up for their small achievements and efforts.

- **ENCOURAGE KIDS TO HAVE THEIR OWN STYLE**: In today's world, children are running behind famous personalities and peers to follow their trend and style. They are not using their mind and cognitive skills to develop their own style and ways. The kids believe that their choices are not worth it and lacks the modern touch, due to which they run behind other people.

To get over this situation, parents should give choices to their children and encourage them for whatever they choose. Expose them to a great selection and let them select their own personal style. This will help them think independently and fashion their own style.

- **LET KIDS EXPLORE THEIR INTERESTS**: Don't force your children to select any particular field or education which doesn't match their style or interest. This would be very discouraging and would end up creating stress and frustration for the child. A study had shown that kids following their own interests had a better outcome rate than other children. Many children had interest of collecting pebbles and many had interest in reading books. Let them explore their interests and allow them to grow happily. Following your desired field will have a successful, happy, and bright future.

- **CONFIDENCE:** (Discussed in the next chapter)
- **AVOID GIVING INSTRUCTIONS:** Assign them a task and let them do it their way. Don't give instructions! Many of the children becomes frustrated when they are given instructions for certain work assigned to them. The child believes that they are being treated as a child and not as a grown up. They don't get the medium to express themselves and explore their cognitive abilities. This all becomes a hindrance for your

child's successful growth and exposure.

For example: Give you child a task and let them do it the way they want. This will help the child to interpret his feelings and desires. He will be able to express himself more to you. Moreover, the child will learn from the decisions he will make. This will allow the child to successfully differentiate between right and wrong. All of this would add up and encourages the child to express himself.

- **<u>LISTEN TO YOUR CHILD'S FEELINGS</u>**: Most of the time, parents are very busy to give time to their children. The children love to share their feelings with their parents. They will approach you several times a day to tell about the way they feel about certain thing or situation. However, if you won't listen to them, they will start hiding their feelings and this will affect the bonding between parents and the child.

Give them time! Sit with them and take interest in their life. Interestingly, listening to your children will help you get to know more about their thoughts and dreams. The child will consider you as a friend than as a parent. In this way, he will show no behavioral issue and will have better bonding with other relations in his life.

"Always be yourself, express yourself, have faith in yourself, do not go out and look for a successful personality and duplicate it." -Bruce Lee.

CHAPTER FOUR "SELF-CONFIDENCE"

In the previous chapters, we have discussed about the ways for expressing thoughts through words. Now, we will look into the matter of self-confidence. As we know, self-confidence is all about self-reliance. It is all about acknowledging the abilities and capabilities in ourselves. In this chapter, we will discuss the impact and importance of self-confidence in our daily life.

It is a fact that self-confidence is all around us. From work to home to relationships, self-confidence is everywhere. How does self-confidence affect our work? The workplace is a battleground where a person shows his capabilities and skills. If the person is unable to express and appreciate his skills, the person will lose the competition at the workplace.

Imagine, you are working at a position in a corporation. The boss of the firm is giving promotion to a person from each department. He sets a criterion over which the promotion will be judged. Now, in your department there are two people only. Both of you are equally intelligent and skillful. However, you lack self-confidence and the other person is brilliant in it. Your colleague will be able to express his expertise to its fullest. He will encourage and motivate himself for that promotion. On the other side, you will be scared as you don't have the ability of self-confidence. You are not sure of yourself and your skills. You will consider yourself less worthy for the promotion. Moreover, there is a great chance that your colleague will convince you that he deserves the promotion more than you.

Workplace is all about fighting for you rights. If you are unable to stand for yourself, you will lose your rank and will never be promoted.

"Successful people have fear, successful people have doubts, and successful people have worries. They just don't let these feelings stop them."–T. Harv Eker.

Self-confidence just don't imply on the professional life, but also in your private life. Are you the head of your family? Or are you the most senior person in your family? If yes, then you should have the material of self-confidence in your personality.

How does self-confidence affect our home? You are a role model in your house for your family members. If you think low of yourself and your conditions, this will have a worse effect on the people of your family. They will also think low of themselves. Let's take a brief example of this situation. Suppose, you are a businessman with high status and potential. All of a sudden, you lose majority of your assets. Now, if you lose hope and the courage in yourself, your family will also lose hope and courage. They will think lower of themselves. Depression will fall and soon worse thinks will start happening. However, if you stay strong and support your family in hard times, there is a chance that you will recover from the lose together. The family's bond will strengthen and there will be no worse-case scenario. Furthermore, the children in the family learns from their elders. If the elders are not self-confident, the children will also be less self-confident. They will not consider themselves as weak and less capable. Therefore, self-confident begins at home.

Self-confidence just don't imply on your private life, but also in your personal life; relationships. I know it sounds weird, but it is a fact. How does self-confidence affect our relationship? Self-confidence is all about believing in yourself. Now, if you don't believe in yourself or you don't think you are worthy enough for something, this creates a barrier in your relationship. Look at the bigger picture and try to understand the effect on relationship by self-confidence.

You will have a limited role in the society. The society will gossip and will think low of you. They will take you for granted and it makes it harder for you to stand up for yourself. When you work on feeling better about yourself and having more confidence, your relationships will branch out. You'll have more friends and work relationships, as well as romantic ones.

"*You're willing to commit yourself to the person who expresses interest in you. You become much less discriminating about who you choose. You may even be willing to put up with behavior that doesn't satisfy you, because you feel lucky to have anyone at all, even though you are aware you are not happy,*" –Dr. Lachmann.

There is a greater chance that you have less energy to put in your relation. To build a successful and strong bond, you should boost up your energy and focus on building a healthy relationship. This will help bolster your self-confidence. If there is low self-confidence, drama becomes inevitable and misunderstanding arises in relationships. It is important in a relationship to express your feeling and ideas, otherwise the relationship turns into a misery and frustration. To maintain a healthy relationship, self-confidence is the key.

In this chapter, we will discuss the tips and tricks for building and enhancing self-confidence. We are already aware of its significance, and so it is essential for us to learn the process of building self-confidence. The following points mentions some great ways to build self-confidence:

- **IDENTIFY YOUR NEGATIVE THOUGHTS:** Your negative thought creates a hindrance in your path to success. As we have learned in the belief system, the negative thoughts are created by the conscious mind and it has a negative effect on the subconscious mind. These negative thoughts can be controlled by our own self. It just requires some motivation and uplifting. To boost and build your self-confidence, one must identify its negative thoughts and convert them into positive ones. Think more positive than negative, give positive thoughts more space in your brain than negative thoughts. The subconscious mind is like a warehouse and filling it up with positivity will boost your self-confidence. Avoid spending time around things that makes you feel bad or lower your self-confidence. Take out some time from your busy routine and mark the things that disturb your peaceful mind. Filter them out and you will observe the happiness in your life.

- **MAINTAIN A POSITIVE SUPPORT NETWORK:** If people keep on discouraging you, you will have low self-confident. Your social pressure and fear will increase and you will not be able to interact much with the outer world. Let's take an example, you are a child whose parents keeps on discouraging their child by saying that the child is not capable and is weak. Even though if the child is all good and perfect, he will feel sad and will have a lower self-confidence. This is just a small example related to motivation. If someone motivates you, you perform better. However, if someone continuously disturb you and discourage you, the person will think negative of himself and will remain in depression. It is recommended to keep a positive support network. Stay in people that help you in your difficult time and stand beside you whenever you need any help. "A person is known by the company he keeps."

- **<u>IDENTIFY YOUR TALENTS AND MAKE A PRODUCTIVE</u>**

LIFESTYLE: Keep yourself involved in your habits and interests. Give yourself permission in taking pride in them. Express yourself through different hidden talents of yours. You will feel unique and accomplished. There is a greater chance that you will find compatible friend in your field of interest. Believe in yourself and start taking pride in yourself. For example, if a person loves singing and music, he will keep himself involved in the activities in his free time. He will have no time to think the negativity around him. Interestingly, he can earn from his interests. This will make him more confident and will make him more relaxed in a hectic life. Moreover, accept the compliments gracefully. If you have a lower level of self-confident, you will find it hard to accept a compliment from somebody. You will think that the person is either lying or mistaken.

- **STOP COMPARING YOURSELF WITH OTHERS**: This is the biggest hindrance in the path to self-confidence. In this world, nobody is equal. Everyone has its own potential, stamina, thinking, capabilities, strategies, etc. Don't make your life as your best friend's life. Think different and make a life as you desire than the desire of the people around you. Try to stand aside from the crowd as it requires self-confidence to be different.

Let's take a brief example, if a child's parents are constantly comparing their child with some other child, there is a chance that the child will follow the other child than perusing his dreams. The child will go against his subconscious mind and will get weaker with time. His self-confidence will shatter with time. Always keep a card that is different from others, this will make you special in the society and will increase your self-confidence.

- **LEARN FROM YOUR MISTAKES**: This is the most important tip in boosting your self-confidence. Ego destroys the personality of the people. Don't let your inner ego destroy your impression in others eyes. If you work on your mistake, you will excel in your life. Don't lose hope by failing at one time. Keep on trying and trying until to succeed in your task. If you don't learn from your mistakes, how will you learn to improve? Think for a minute, is it possible to achieve something without even trying for it? No! This is not how the things work. You have to put an effort in the tasks you do. If you learn from your mistakes, you will grow more confident. You will be able to express and face the people with more confidence. There is a great chance that you will learn something unique while improving your mistakes. In this way, your extra knowledge will increase. People will appreciate you for your knowledge and wisdom. Learning from mistakes is the golden key in boosting the self-confidence.

"Each time we face our fear, we gain strength, courage, and confidence in the doing." –Theodore Roosevelt.

CONCLUSION

In the light of the above stated points, it can be concluded that children are a great asset that needs a great amount of attention for better growth of themselves and the nation. Nowadays, children are under constant stress and pressure of studies, friends, financial crisis, etc. They look around for mind peace and comfort, but fails which leaves a huge impact on their nature and behavior.

There are many factors that needs to be considered when teaching a child about the world and its cruelties. The significant factors are: Mindfulness, gratitude, confidence, and ability to express themselves. These factors are very much implemented in every phase of life and asks for great attention.

Gratitude is extremely necessary to have a happy life and soul. This makes you feel alive and burden free. Confidence helps you believe in yourself and your abilities. It allows you to excel in every matter of life; workplace, relationship, etc. Mindfulness allows the child to remain calm and relaxed. In this chaotic world, it is a great way to remove the negativity out of the mind. Expressing yourself allows you to represent yourself on many platforms and be amongst the highest of the society.

Gratitude, confidence, mindfulness, and the ability to express yourself are some qualities that can brighten the future of any person. Listen to your children and help them get along with their problems and complexities. Keep on encouraging them and motivate them to perform better in life.

Let there be no stop for your child's growth and success. Move from authoritarian parenting methods to authoritative parenting practices. Teach your child to stop procrastinating and start focusing for better and healthy life.

"Children will listen to you after they feel listened to." -Jane Nelson.

DISCLAIMER

All information posted is merely for educational and informational purposes. It is not intended as a substitute for professional advice. Should you decide to act upon any information on this website, you do so at your own risk.

While the information on this website has been verified to the best of our abilities, we cannot guarantee that there are no mistakes or errors.

We reserve the right to change this policy at any given time, of which you will be promptly updated. If you want to make sure that you are up to date with the latest changes, we advise you to frequently visit this page.

PERSONAL NOTES